ORIGAMI
BOXES
and more!

Florence Temko

TUTTLE PUBLISHING

Boston • Rutland, Vermont • Tokyo

ACKNOWLEDGMENTS

I owe a debt of gratitude to many friends in the international origami community who, over many years, have always been ready to share their interest in paperfolding. I wish I could name everyone, but regret that is impossible. The boxes in this book are either traditional, my own designs, or created by designers who have been credited. Some designs may be similar to ones that have been created by others but whose names may no longer be distinguishable. I am very grateful to those who have patiently participated in the time-consuming task of testing the directions and offered their general encouragement and support: John Andrisan; Tyler and Yolanda Anyon; Sharon Brengel; Jim Cowley; V'Ann Cornelius (Vice President of OrigamiUSA); Arlene Edelstein; Dorothy Engleman, Tanya Dean; Charlie De Stefano; Alexandra Hirsh; Erin Hook; Judith Jaskowiak; Cath Kachur; David Lister (former President of the British Origami Society); George Ondovachak; Dane Petersen; Nancy Petersen; Lisa and Mark Saliers; David, Dennis, Janet, Perri and Rachel Temko; Arnold Tubis. Not least Jennifer Lantagne and Helen Watt (supportive editors).

First published in 2004 by Tuttle Publishing, an imprint of Periplus Editions (HK) Ltd., with editorial offices at 153 Milk Street, Boston, Massachusetts 02109.

Copyright © 2004 by Florence Temko

Library of Congress Cataloging-in-Publication Data
Temko, Florence.
    Origami boxes and more / Florence Temko — 1st. ed.
      p. cm.
    ISBN 0-8048-3495-4 (pbk.)
    1. Box making. 2. Origami. I. Title.
TT870.5.T46 2004
736'.982--dc21   2003050716

Distributed by

North America, Latin America, and Europe
Tuttle Publishing
Distribution Center
Airport Industrial Park
364 Innovation Drive
North Clarendon, VT 05759-9436
Tel: (802) 773-8930
Fax: (802) 773-6993
Email: info@tuttlepublishing.com
Website: www.tuttlepublishing.com

Japan
Tuttle Publishing
Yaekari Building, 3F
5-4-12 Ōsaki, Shinagawa-ku
Tokyo 141-0032
Tel: (03) 5437-0171
Fax: (03) 5437-0755
Email: tuttle-sales@gol.com

Asia Pacific
Berkeley Books Pte. Ltd.
130 Joo Seng Road
#06-0103 Olivine Building
Singapore 368357
Tel: (65) 6280-3320
Fax: (65) 6280-6290
Email: inquiries@periplus.com.sg

First Edition
09 08 07 06 05 04 9 8 7 6 5 4 3 2 1

Text design by Linda Carey
Illustrations by Clay Fernald and Daniel P. Brennan based on original diagrams by Florence Temko
Photographs by Dave Kutchukian
Printed in Singapore

CONTENTS

For ease of reference, standard origami terms (except mountain and valley folds) are listed under the project where they occur.

◣ Introduction

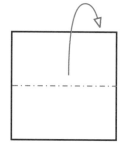

Folding paper boxes has recently become a popular branch of origami. Crafters seem to derive great satisfaction in seeing a box develop step by step, besides enjoying the obvious, practical result.

Boxes may be folded from one sheet of paper, or assembled from separate units, called modules. In *Origami Boxes and More*, I have tried to offer a representative selection of both techniques. The usefulness of origami boxes is quite evident. An attractive box enhances any gift presented in it, while the box itself may become a gift that the recipient can keep as a home accessory. Open containers can be stacked with candy, toiletries, or other things, then swathed in cellophane gathered at the top and tied with a ribbon. Open boxes turned on their sides can serve as three-dimensional frames for any figures displayed inside. A series of boxes can help organize unsightly areas or they can be displayed as ornaments or table decorations. In my studio, a mobile of five boxes in bright colors hovers over my computer.

But boxes also present mystery. Some artists hide objects inside, stimulating visitors to use their imagination to visualize different contents. The ancient Greek story of Pandora's box illustrates the irresistible temptation to explore the contents of a closed container.

You are invited to select from the shapes and sizes of boxes illustrated in this book, combine them with beautiful papers, and end up with your own handcrafted surprises.

◣ About Origami Techniques

To help you make sense of the lines and arrows on the drawings, you should study the explanations of a few basic techniques. It will be well worth a few minutes to learn to recognize the following procedures which are international standards for origami.

Basic Procedures

1. Valley Fold

In general, you can fold paper toward you or away from you. In origami, the forward crease is called a valley fold. In the diagrams it is shown by a line of dashes.

Fold the square in half by bringing one edge of the paper toward you and matching it to the opposite edge.

You have made a valley fold.

With this one simple fold you have made a greeting card.

Happy Birthday!

2. Mountain Fold

When you crease paper to the back, away from you, it's called a mountain fold. In the diagrams it is shown by a line of dashes and dots.

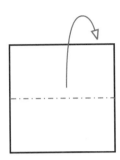

Fold the square in half by guiding one edge of the paper to the back and matching it to the opposite edge.

You have made a mountain fold. With this one simple fold, you have made a tent.

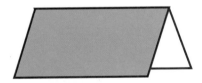

3. Existing Crease

A crease made previously is shown in the diagrams by a thin line that does not touch the edges.

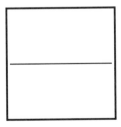

4. Arrows

In the diagrams you will see four kinds of arrows. They indicate the direction in which to fold.

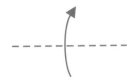

Make a valley fold.

Make a mountain fold.

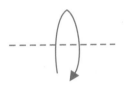

Double Arrow—Fold and unfold the same crease.

Curly Arrow—Turn the paper over.

5. Reverse Fold

One of the most common moves is called a reverse fold.

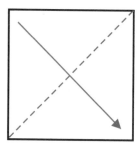

1. Fold a small square from corner to corner.

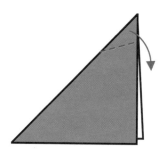

2. Place the paper exactly as shown. Fold the top corner over to the right, so that it peeks over the open edge.

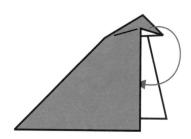

3a. Let the paper open up, and swing the corner of the paper in between the two layers of paper on the crease you made in step 2.

3b. Close up the paper.

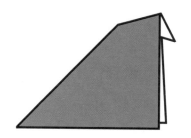

4. Completed reverse fold.

The instructions for making a reverse fold are indicated with a dash-dot-dash line, the same as for a mountain fold, but the text states that you must make a reverse fold.

You may wonder why this procedure is called a "reverse" fold: In step 2 you see that the doubled paper is made up of a mountain fold on the front layer and a valley fold on the back layer. After you have pushed the corner in between the two layers of paper in step 3 you have "reversed" the valley fold into a mountain fold.

About Bases

Many origami models begin with the same series of steps, which are called bases. They are recognized by paperfolders all over the world. In

Origami Boxes and More, bases occur in the following models:

- ❏ *Square or Preliminary Base*: Desktop Basket, Star Basket
- ❏ *Triangle or Waterbomb Base*: Round Bowl
- ❏ *Blintz Base*: Classic Japanese Box, Five Happiness Bowl, Four Thirsty Birds
- ❏ *Frog Base*: Round Bowl

How to Cut Paper Squares

Many of the projects in this book begin with a square piece of paper. All sides are of equal length and all corners are right (90-degree) angles. Paper can be squared on a board paper cutter, if available, but it's quite easy to cut any rectangular sheet into a square:

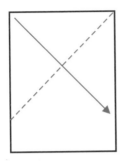

1. Fold a short edge to a long edge.

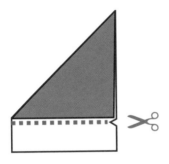

2. Cut off the extra rectangle.

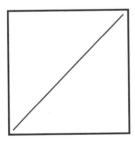

3. A square.

Sheets of 8½" x 11" copy and other printing papers can be cut into two sizes:

- ❏ With one cut, you will have squares 8½" sides.
- ❏ With two cuts, you will have two squares with 5½" sides.

Copy shops will usually cut a whole ream of paper for a small fee. A ream will provide five hundred 8½" squares or a thousand 5½" squares.

Helpful Tips

If you are having trouble with a step, check the following:

1. Make sure you distinguish carefully between a valley fold (dashed line) and a mountain fold (dash-dot-dash line).

2. Be sure to observe the curly arrow asking you to turn the paper over.

3. Compare your paper to the illustrations for:
   - ❏ the step you are working on;
   - ❏ the step before; and
   - ❏ the next one, which is your goal.

4. Read the directions out loud.

Diagrams

The darker shading on the diagrams indicates the colored side of the paper, if you are using paper which is colored on one side only.

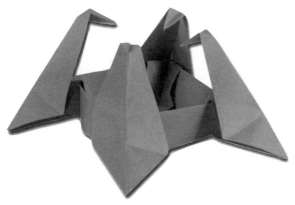

For the sake of clarity, the illustrations may increase in size from the beginning of the project to the end. But the angles are always consistent, and you can test your own paper against them.

Measurements

Measurements are given in inches and centimeters, but they may not always be exactly equal, in order to avoid awkward fractions. In some cases specific sizes are recommended, but in most cases you may use smaller or larger pieces of paper.

About Paper

A variety of papers are suitable for making boxes. Many of the boxes in this book can be folded either from American-size letter paper, 8½" x 11" or A4-size letter paper, 210 mm x 297 mm. Origami squares and gift wrap will give pleasing results, but for large boxes, stiffer papers, like Canson mi-teintes and wallpapers, will add stability. Local wallpaper stores will usually provide outdated sample books for free. Select pages with the least plastic coating. These thick papers are harder to crease sharply, but a folding tool will make it easier on your fingers. These tools can be found in art supply and craft stores, but an ice-cream stick or something similar will work equally well to help you produce crisp-looking boxes.

Origami Paper

Ready-cut squares in varying sizes and colors are available in some art, museum and gift stores, and from catalogs. They are usually colored on one side and white on the other.

Computer and Bond Paper; Printing Paper in Bright Colors

These kinds of papers are available in a large assortment of colors at copy shops, office supply stores, and school suppliers. They are sold in reams (packages of 500 sheets), available in two weights (described on the package wrapping): 20 lbs. or 24 lbs. Printing papers are most economical for schools, youth groups, and other large groups.

Gift Wrap Paper

It is quite difficult to cut paper from rolls into specific sizes, but very worthwhile for special results.

Handmade Paper

These papers are softer, but give rich-looking results. Japanese washi paper in glorious patterns is available in sheets or packages of squares.

Paper Colored on Both Sides

Some projects look better when made from paper that is colored on both sides, such as printing papers.

Duo-colored origami squares are sold in packets and have different colors on the front and the back.

You can make your own fancy duo papers by gluing sheets of gift wrap or other papers back to back with spray glue or glue sticks. This will add strength to boxes.

Recycled Paper

Out-of-date flyers, magazine covers, and other discarded papers can be turned into colorful boxes.

The kind of recreational origami now popular in Asia and Western countries began in the late nineteenth century, but received its greatest impetus in the latter half of the twentieth century. The Japanese paperfolder Tomoke Fuse may be credited as the most original and prolific creator of origami boxes.

Why fold paper?

Many people find pleasure in the folding process itself, by following diagrams; others can't wait to achieve the results. Almost all paperfolders enjoy giving away objects they have folded, either on the spur of the moment or as elegant gifts.

▲ FAQ (Frequently Asked Questions)

What is the history of paperfolding?

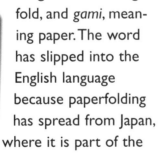

"Origami" is a Japanese word consisting of *ori* meaning to fold, and *gami*, meaning paper. The word has slipped into the English language because paperfolding has spread from Japan, where it is part of the culture. It is known that paper has been folded in Japan for ceremonial purposes since the twelfth century and that paper began to be folded for decorative use and entertainment in the sixteenth century.

Records show that paper was folded in Europe in the fourteenth century. In the sixteenth and seventeenth centuries, it was common practice to fold square baptismal certificates in set patterns.

Is origami creative?

The fun of origami can be increased by going beyond simply following existing directions to creating new designs. After you have folded a few boxes, you will become familiar with some of the basics of paperfolding. You may want to introduce your own variations, which may appear in just minutes, like a doodle, or you can set out to create an entirely new design. Many paperfolders enjoy the challenge of inventing their own models.

In another variation, some crafters use stiffened fabric instead of paper.

How long does it take to learn origami?

A simple model can be learned in just a few minutes, while a complex one may present a challenge for many hours. The boxes in this book are in the simple to intermediate range of difficulty.

How can I teach others?

After they know how to fold a box, most people like to share the secret with others. It is one thing to teach someone in an informal setting; it is quite another to give a program to a class or other group. Before any formal presentation:

- ☐ Decide clearly what you would like to teach;
- ☐ Make sure you know how to fold the models, making them again and again until you are familiar with them, verbalizing each step to yourself;
- ☐ Prepare the quantity and types of papers you will need, including larger squares for demonstrating in front of a group.

What is origami language?

If we accept one dictionary definition of the word *language* as "any mode of communication," then origami itself is a language. When paperfolders find themselves in situations where they have no common language with other people, they often fold and give away an origami bird or toy. They are communicating very well, eliciting smiles and friendship.

In addition, some procedures involving several steps are described in one simple term. "Reverse fold" is an example. In the instructions for *Origami Boxes and More* I have referred to these shortcuts as "origami language."

Where do models originate?

There are three sources:

- ☐ *Traditional:* In many cultures toys are folded from paper, like the dart airplane or the hat made from a newspaper.
- ☐ *Known creators:* When paperfolders show or teach models by known creators they always credit them by name.
- ☐ *Unknown creators:* When a model is handed around informally at parties, in schools, and elsewhere, the name of the creator may unfortunately become lost in the shuffle.

What are crease patterns?

Directions for origami models are usually shared step by step, as in this book. In a recent development, paperfolders are using "crease patterns" instead. Crease patterns show the lines that remain on a flat paper sheet after a model has been been folded and then unfolded completely. Some paperfolders consider folding complex origami models from crease patterns to be a technical challenge. A creator may even map out a folding pattern before actually taking a piece of paper in hand.

As an example of this method, you can try to fold the All-Purpose Box from this crease pattern.

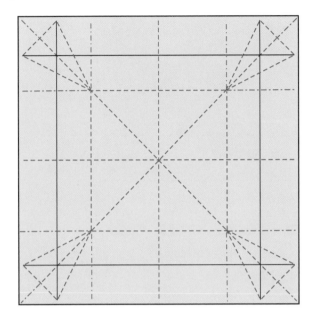

What about copyrights?

You may fold any origami and photocopy printed instructions for your own personal use. You cannot include them in handouts or any printed or electronic format without permission from the creator or copyright holder, which may be a publisher. For more detailed information, consult the guidelines provided by OrigamiUSA (see address below).

How can I meet other paperfolders?

It's great fun to meet with other paperfolders. You will be welcomed at origami clubs that exist in many localities. Members of all ages usually meet monthly to exchange directions for models and share other information.

OrigamiUSA holds an annual convention in New York City that is attended by more than 600 enthusiasts from many countries. Other conventions take place in different places.

Further Information

Readers interested in learning more about paperfolding can use the keyword "origami" on the Internet. These American and British groups can connect you with other paperfolders in your area or your country:

OrigamiUSA
15 West 77th Street
New York, NY 10024
USA
Website: www.origami-usa.org

British Origami Society
c/o Penny Groom
2A The Chestnuts
Countesthorpe, Leicester
LE8 5TL, United Kingdom
Website: www.britishorigami.org.uk

◤ About Boxes

Containers are among the earliest historical artifacts, as they are necessary to everyday life. Among their many uses, boxes were the repositories of important family documents and other valuables for safe keeping. In Great Britain their importance is celebrated as a national holiday called Boxing Day on December 26, the day after Christmas. The term refers to the centuries-old custom of filling boxes with gifts of clothing and money for employees and the poor on that day.

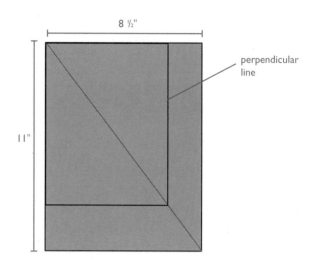

The Geometry of Boxes

Origami is increasingly being recognized as an educational tool, helpful in augmenting curriculum requirements in math and science. Teachers especially like to use the underlying geometry of boxes, as they have found that students absorb the relevant math principles more easily, because origami is fun.

How to Size Boxes

The same folding pattern can be followed to make a tiny box for a pair of earrings or a bigger box for a dozen cookies.

If you want to make a box in a size different than suggested in the instructions, you need only to begin with a smaller or larger piece of paper in the same proportion, then follow the same folding pattern.

Here is a method by which you can maintain the proportion without a mathematical calculation. Let us assume the instructions call for an 8½" x 11" piece of paper, but you would like to make a smaller box.

- ❑ On an 8½" piece of paper draw a diagonal line from the top left corner to the bottom right corner.
- ❑ From the top edge draw a vertical line to the diagonal.
- ❑ From the end of the vertical line draw a horizontal line to the outside edge.

The two lines will define the new piece of paper. For bigger sizes, place the original piece of paper on a larger piece of paper and extend the diagonal.

Covered Boxes

A lid should fit snugly on top of a box. Achieving this may require some experimentation by varying the difference in the dimensions of the lid and the bottom. Generally, a difference of $1/4$" between the two pieces works well, but the thickness of the paper often has an effect. In the instructions in this book, I have tried to be as precise as possible.

Strengthening

You can stiffen boxes by cutting two pieces of cardboard to fit inside the bottom and the lid. Or you can bond the paper to a piece of plain paper, as suggested under "Paper Colored on Both Sides."

EASIEST BOX

This box is undoubtedly one of the most widely known origami designs, as it is often taught in schools and elsewhere. It can be made from any letter-size paper, recycled flyer, or colorful cover of a magazine.

You need:

A piece of paper, 8½" x 11" (or A4)

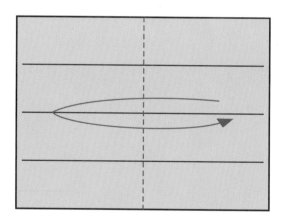

1a. Fold the paper in half the long way.
1b. Unfold the paper flat.

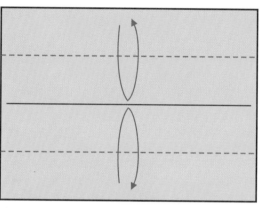

2a. Fold both long edges to the crease.
2b. Unfold the paper flat.

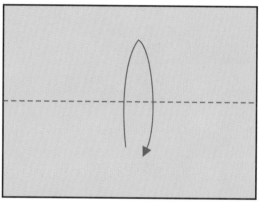

3a. Fold the paper in half the short way.
3b. Unfold the paper flat.

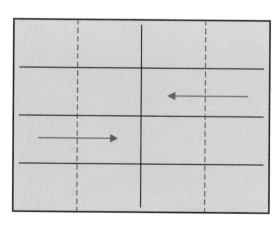

4. Fold both short edges to the crease. Do not unfold. In Origami language this is called a book fold.

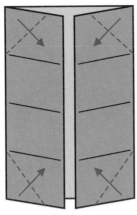

5. Fold all four corners to the nearest creases going across. The corners do not reach all the way to the middle.

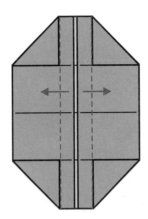

6. Fold the two cut edges in the middle of the paper as far as you can over the folded corners. Make these creases very sharp, as they will be holding the box together.

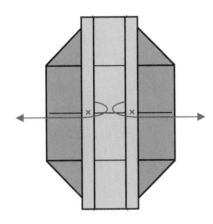

7. The folding of the box is complete, but where is it? If you pull the box apart at the two Xs, it will appear magically.

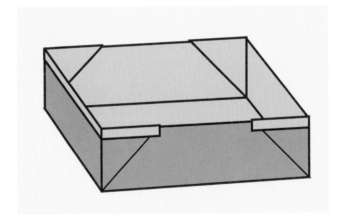

8. Completed Easiest Box
For a crisper look, crease all four corners sharply.

Covered Box

For a covered box fold two boxes exactly alike. One will fit over the other. But if you are using construction or other heavier paper, cut ¹⁄₄" (5 mm) off one long and one short edge for folding the bottom of the box.

ALL-PURPOSE BOX

I have called this the All-Purpose Box because it is easy to fold and can be made in any desired size.

You need:

Two paper squares of the same size
Scissors

If paper is colored on only one side, begin with the white side facing up.

FOR THE BOTTOM OF THE BOX

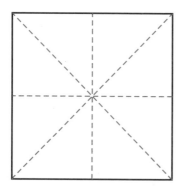

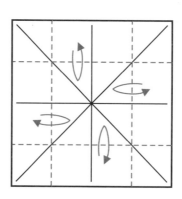

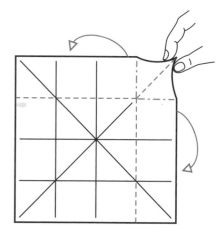

Ia. Fold one square in half both ways. Unfold the paper each time.

Ib. Fold on both diagonals. Unfold each time.

2. Fold all four edges to the middle creases. Unfold the paper each time.

3a. Pinch the diagonal crease at one corner, so that the sides of the box rise up.

3b. Repeat on the other three corners.

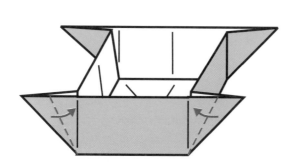

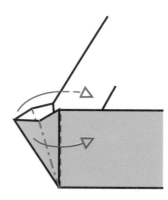

4. On the triangles that stick out at each corner, bring the folded diagonal edges to the nearby upright creases. Unfold each time.

5. View of one corner. Separate the two layers of the corner and spread them around the side of the box.

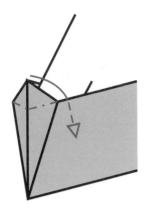

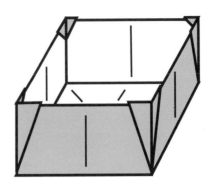

6a. Tuck the triangle at the top into the inside of the box with a firm crease, as this holds the box together. Also crease the upright sharply.

6b. Repeat steps 5 and 6a on the other three corners.

7. Completed Bottom of the Box

FOR THE LID

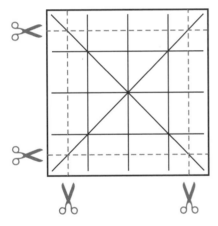

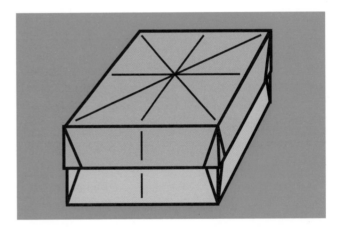

1a. With the second square, follow steps 1 and 2 exactly as for the first square.

1b. Fold each of the four edges to the nearest crease. Unfold the paper each time.

1c. Cut on the four creases you just made.

2a. Follow the instructions for steps 3 through 6 for folding the bottom of the box.

2b. Put the lid and bottom of the box together

2c. Completed All-Purpose Box

Sizes: It is easy to make an All-Purpose Box in a specific size. The dimensions of the final box will always be half the size of the beginning square. For example, an 8" (20 cm) square will produce a 4" (10 cm) box.

Rectangular Box: The same folding method can be used to create a rectangular box. Begin with a rectangle of paper. Fold it in half, lengthwise. Fold the two long edges to the middle crease, which will determine the height of the box. Fold the short edges to the same height. Now follow the rest of the instructions for folding the square All-Purpose Box starting at step 3.

Reinforcement: Spots of glue will hold the small triangles inside the corners more securely.

ROW OF BOXES

For a neat desktop, make a row of connected boxes to store paper clips, rubber bands, and other small items. The instructions suggest three boxes in a row, but you can make as many as you like. The number depends only on the length of the strip of paper you use.

You need:

A strip of paper 12" x 4" (30 cm x 10 cm)
If the paper is colored on only one side, begin with white side facing up.

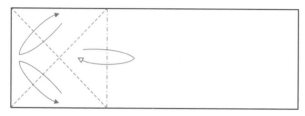

1a. At one end of the strip, valley fold the short edge to the long edge, through the corner. Unfold the paper flat.

1b. Valley fold the short edge to the opposite long edge. Unfold the paper flat.

1c. You have an X on the paper. Make a mountain fold, to the back, at the end of the X. Unfold the paper flat.

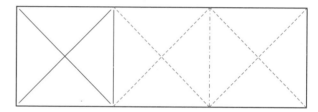

2. Repeat the three folds for the length of the strip, making two more Xs.

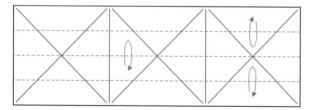

3a. Valley fold the strip in half the long way. Unfold the paper.

3b. Fold both long edges to the middle crease. Unfold the paper.

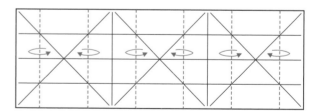

4. Fold both short edges and the two mountain folds to the middle of the three Xs. Unfold each time.

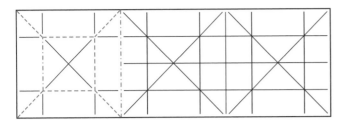

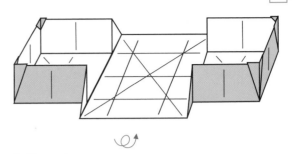

5a. Raise the sides of the box at one end around its center square.

5b. Two corners will stick out at the end of the paper. Fold them as you did in steps 4, 5, and 6 of the All-Purpose Box.

5c. Repeat steps 5a and 5b at the other end of the strip.

6. Turn the paper over.

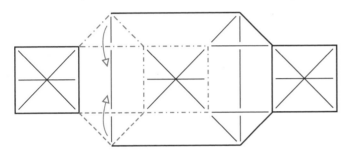

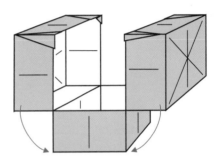

7a. Outline the middle box by making four mountain folds.

7b. At the left side of the middle box, two corners stick out. At both corners, mountain fold the two slanted creases and valley fold the corner toward the middle of the paper with a sharp crease. In origami language, this is called a reverse fold.

7c. Repeat steps 7a and 7b on the right side.

8. Line up the boxes in a flat row.

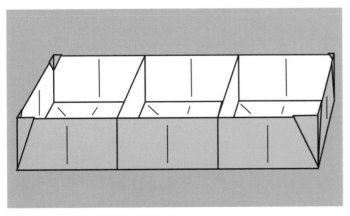

9. Completed Row of Boxes

Sizes: The three boxes are each 2" (5 cm) square. For each added box, add 4" (10 cm) to the length of the original paper strip.

For bigger boxes, increase the width and length of the strip. The finished boxes will be half the width of the paper.

Reinforcement: The boxes will lie flat when filled with paper clips and other small things. Or you can glue the sides of the boxes together.

DESKTOP BASKET

Use this simple container to collect the oddments that tend to accumulate, but often have no place to go. A square cut from a sheet of stationery will do nicely, or you can cut a larger square from gift wrap.

You need:

A paper square

If paper is colored on only one side, begin with the colored side facing up.

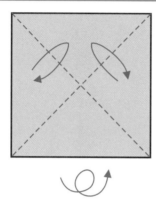

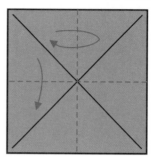

1a. Fold the square from corner to corner in both directions. Unfold the paper flat each time.

1b. Turn the paper over.

2a. Fold the paper in half and unfold.

2b. Fold the paper in half the other way and leave it folded.

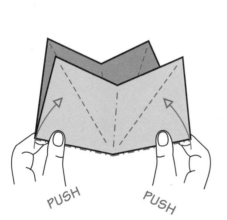

PUSH PUSH

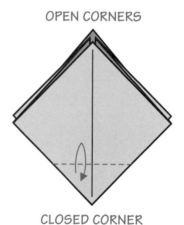

OPEN CORNERS

CLOSED CORNER

3. Grasp the paper with both hands at the folded edge in the exact positions shown in the diagram. Move your hands up and toward each other in the direction of the arrows until the paper is formed into a square. Place it flat on the table.

4a. Make sure the square has two flaps on each side. If you have only one flap on one side and three flaps on the other, flip one flap over. In origami language, this is called the square or preliminary base.

4b. Place the square with the closed corner pointing towards you.

4c. Fold the closed corner up, as shown: first to the front, then to the back, and unfold.

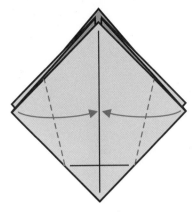

5a. Fold the two outside corners on the top layer to the middle crease. Note the folds start at the crease made in step 4.

5b. Repeat on the back.

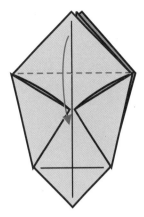

6a. Fold the top corner of the front layer down.

6b. Turn the model over and repeat on the back.

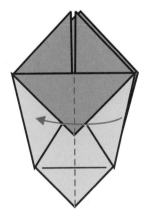

7a. Fold the right flap over to the left, like turning the page of a book. In origami language, this is called a book fold.

7b. Turn the model over and repeat on the back, again folding the flap from right to left.

7c. Fold the top corner down.

7d. Repeat on the back.

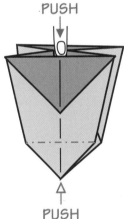

PUSH

PUSH

8. Reach inside and flatten the bottom of the basket on the horizontal lines made in step 4. Sharpen them neatly from the outside.

Party Hat: For an instant party hat, turn the basket upside down and add a feather or other decoration.

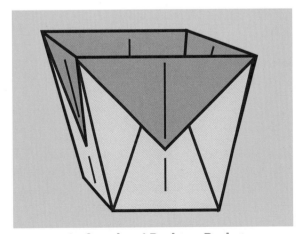

9. Completed Desktop Basket

21

CLASSIC JAPANESE BOX

You need:

Two paper squares of the same size

If paper is colored on only one side, begin with the colored side facing up.

FOR THE BOTTOM OF THE BOX

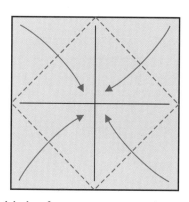

1a. Fold one square in half both ways. Unfold each time.

1b. Turn the paper over.

2. Fold the four corners to the middle.

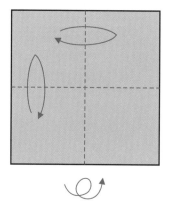

3. In origami language, this is called a blintz base. Fold the four edges to the middle. Unfold each time.

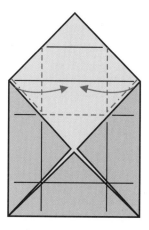

4. Lift up one flap. Pinch in the right corner with a mountain fold, and push it over to the left. Now pinch in the left corner and push it over to the right.

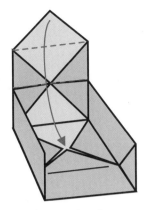

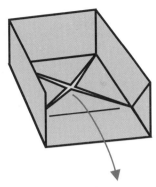

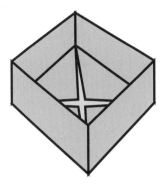

5. Bring down the flap, into the inside of the box, locking in both corners. The sides of the box will stand up.

6. Lift up the flap on the opposite side of the box and lock in the other two corners in the same way.

7. Completed bottom of the box. Sharpen all creases for a crisp look.

FOR THE LID OF THE BOX

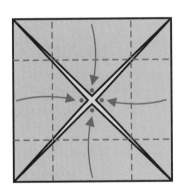

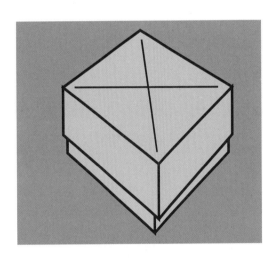

1a. Fold the second square through the first two steps in exactly the same way as for the bottom of the box. In step 3, fold the edges of the paper not all the way to the middle, but instead leave a narrow gap of ⅛" (2.5 mm). Unfold each time. This allows for the extra space needed for the lid to fit over the bottom of the box.

1b. Continue with steps 4, 5, and 6 for the bottom of the box.

2a. Fit the lid on top of the bottom of the box.

2b. Completed Classic Japanese Box

BANDED BOX

The Banded Box looks as though it is wrapped with ribbon, but it is in fact folded from a single square. As this box is a variation of the simpler Classic Japanese Box, it is helpful to practice making one of those first.

You need two squares of the same size, but the second square (for the bottom of the box) has to be trimmed, as stated in the directions.

You need:

Two 10" (25 cm) paper squares
Scissors

FOR THE LID OF THE BOX

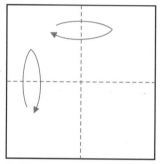

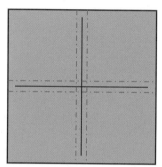

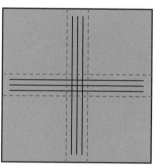

1a. Fold the paper in half both ways.

1b. Unfold the paper after each fold.

2. If the paper is colored on only one side, place the colored side up. Make mountain folds ¼" (5 mm) away from both sides of the two creases. Unfold each time.

3a. Make valley folds ¼" (5 mm) away from both side of the four mountain folds. Unfold the paper each time.

3b. Pleat both bands of four creases on the existing valley and mountain folds, as shown in the profile view.

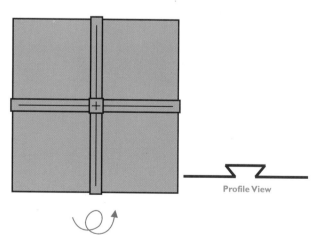

Profile View

4. Turn the paper over.

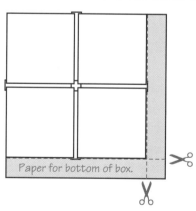

Paper for bottom of box.

5a. Now trim the second square to the same size as the folded square.

5b. Then cut another ¼" (5 mm) off two adjacent edges of the second square.

5c. Set it aside for the bottom of the box.

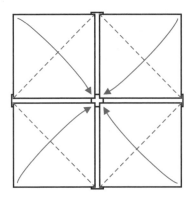

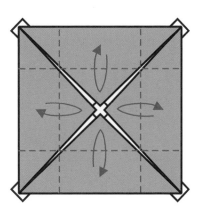

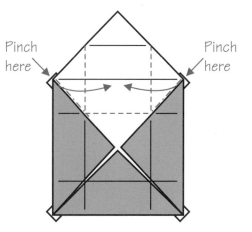

6. Back to the lid. Fold the four corners to the middle.

7. Fold the four edges to the middle. Unfold each time.

8. Lift up one flap. Pinch in the right corner with a mountain fold, and push it over to the left. Now pinch in the left corner and push it over to the right.

Pinch here

Pinch here

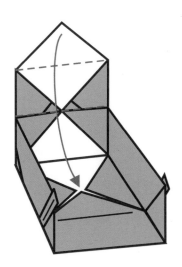

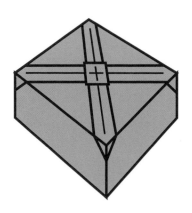

FOR THE BOTTOM OF THE BOX

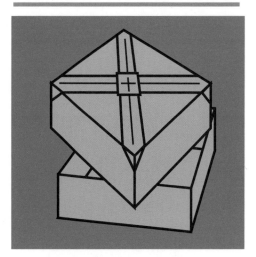

9. Bring down the flap into the inside of the box, locking in both corners. The sides of the box will stand up. Lift up the flap on the opposite side of the box and lock in the other two corners in the same way.

10. Completed lid of the box. Sharpen all creases.

11a. With the second square, follow the directions for folding the bottom of the Classic Japanese Box.

11b. Fit the lid and bottom of the box together.

11c. **Completed Banded Box**

NESTED BOXES

Several boxes that fit inside each other make welcome gifts. Recipients can use them as gift boxes or keep them on display for friends who will probably be fascinated with them, taking them apart, stacking them into a tower, and reassembling them to disappear inside the largest box.

You can make a set of four nested boxes from eight squares in graduated sizes, or a bigger stack from more squares.

You need:

Eight paper squares, in sizes 3", 3¹/₂", 4", 4¹/₂", 5", 5¹/₂", 6", and 6¹/₂" (8 cm, 9 cm, 10 cm, 11 cm, 12 cm, 13 cm, 14 cm, and 15 cm)

1. Fold all eight squares following the directions for the six steps for the bottom of the Classic Japanese Box.

2. Fit the two smallest pieces into a lidded box. Then fit the two boxes in the next bigger sizes around them. Follow with the next two bigger ones, and finally the two largest ones.

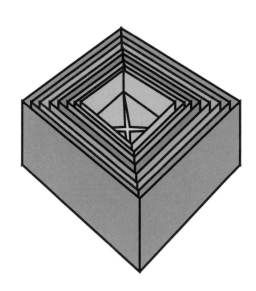

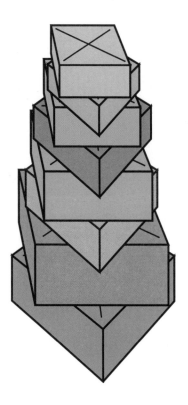

Papers: The appropriate selection of papers is important in creating an appealing series of boxes. For the stack of seven boxes shown in the photo I chose sheets from a book of gift wrap papers with Japanese themes. In this way, the colors relate, but each box has a different pattern.

PLANT POT COVER

This pot disguise is woven from strips of newspaper, using a traditional basket-making technique. You can substitute gift wrap for a more colorful effect. You can make larger baskets with more and longer strips. The strips can be extended by interweaving or gluing the ends together.

Weaving baskets, hats, roses, and other things with paper strips or palm fronds is an ancient craft, closely related to origami.

You need:

Twelve pieces of newsprint, each approx. 6" x 22" (15 cm x 55 cm)
Ruler, Paper clips, Scissors, Glue

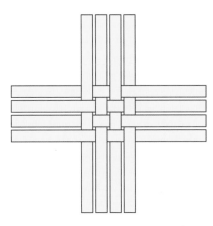

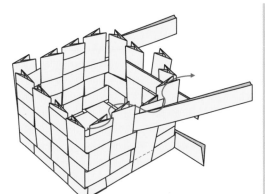

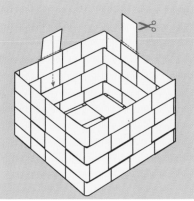

1a. Fold each piece in half lengthwise, three times, making eight layers. Firm up the creases by running a ruler over the strips.

1b. Interweave eight of the strips, as shown.

2a. Bend all sixteen ends upright around the central weaving.

2b. Weave the remaining four strips around the sides, as shown. You can hold them in place temporarily with paper clips.

3a. Fold the ends of the strips into the inside of the basket.

3b. Tuck the ends into the closest opening or glue them down, trimming the ends off as needed.

4. **Completed Plant Pot Cover**

Patterns: The simple "over-one, under-one" pattern is only one of many weaving patterns you can achieve. Here are just a few ideas for diversifying the weaving technique: use more strips, narrower strips, or different widths. You can also vary the "over-one, under-one" pattern, using "over-one, under-two" and other combinations.

Make a Box with a Lid: You can weave a lid with the same technique as for the box, using only two strips in step 2, instead of four. The lid will usually fit if you interweave the strips in step 2 just slightly more loosely.

BOX OF CARDS

Don't throw out an old deck of cards—convert it into table decorations for your next card, or other party. This design also works with index cards, postcards, and photographs.

You need:

Eighteen playing cards

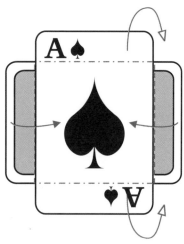

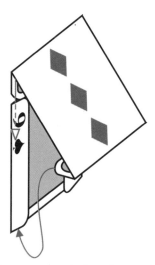

1a. Place the backs of two cards across each other, as shown.

1b. Fold the ends over the center sections, away from the front of each card.

2. Separate the two cards but keep them folded. Slide one of the ends in between the ends of the other card. Do the same with the opposite end. You will have a square with all four ends hidden inside.

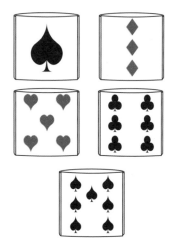

3. Fold four more pairs of cards in the same way.

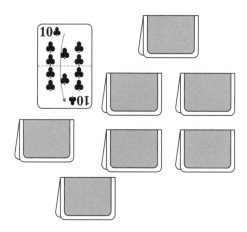

4. Fold the remaining eight cards in half, the short way.

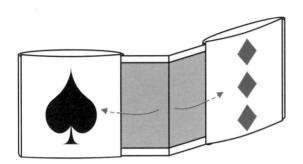

5a. Slide a folded card into the side openings of two squares.

5b. Connect two more squares with them in the same way to form a ring.

6. Use the other four folded cards to lock in the last square as the bottom of the box.

7. Completed Box of Cards

For a Lid: Place another pair of cards on top of the box and connect it with a folded card.

Other Shapes: You can create rectangular boxes using more units made up of pairs of cards, or make triangle boxes, using fewer units.

PATCHWORK BOX

The bottom and lid of this modular box are each made up of four separate units. The box was invented by Laura Kruskal, who teaches origami to university audiences in many countries during her frequent travels. Sometimes she prepares gifts for her hosts by folding boxes ahead of time, carrying them flat in her luggage, ready to fill them with candy or other small items upon arrival.

You need:

Four pieces of paper, 8½" x 11"
Four pieces of paper 8½" x 10½"
This box also works with 9" x 12" construction paper, or with A4 paper if you cut off 3 cm from one of the short edges.

If the paper is colored on only one side, begin with the colored side facing up.
The lid and bottom of the box are folded in the same way.

FOLDING EACH UNIT

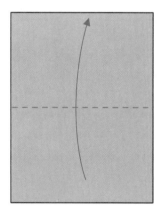

1. Fold the short bottom edge to the top edge.

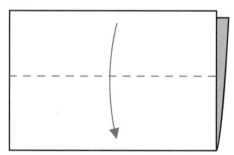

2. Fold the top layer down to the folded edge.

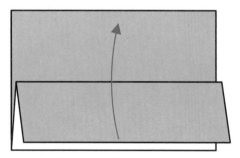

3. Unfold step 2.

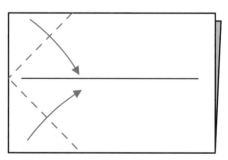

4. On the left side, fold the single layer of the top corner and the bottom corner to the middle crease.

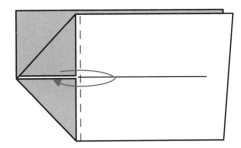

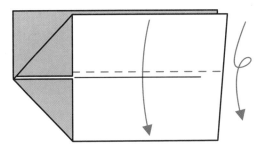

5a. Valley fold along the edges of the triangles.
5b. Unfold this crease.

6a. Fold one layer down.
6b. Turn the paper over, flipping the top to the bottom.

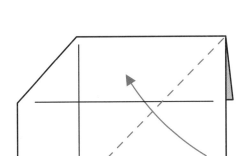

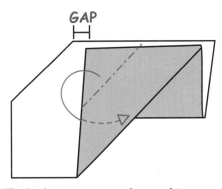

7. Fold the entire bottom right corner over to the top edge.

8. Tuck the corner under, making a mountain fold.

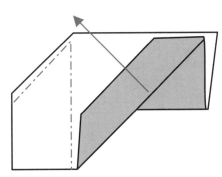

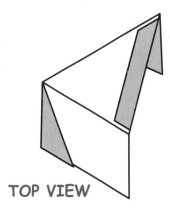

TOP VIEW

9. Shape the unit by lifting up the slanted edge.

10. A completed unit. Fold seven more units.

PATCHWORK BOX

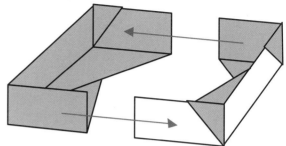

ASSEMBLY

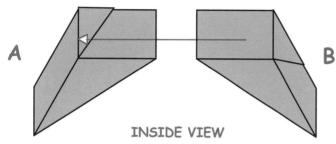

INSIDE VIEW

1a. Each unit forms one corner. Combine two of the smaller units. On the inside of unit A you will see a triangular pocket. Slide the straight edge on the left side of unit B into that pocket.

1b. Repeat with two more units.

2a. Slide the two combined pieces into each other, repeating the locking procedure. Let the triangles on the inside rotate in a counterclockwise manner. Push all four units tightly together.

2b. Crease all edges sharply.

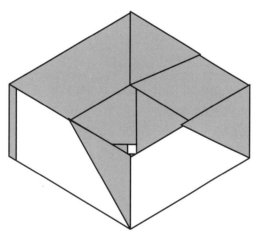

3a. Completed box bottom.

3b. Assemble the four other units into the box lid. Place it on top of the bottom of the box.

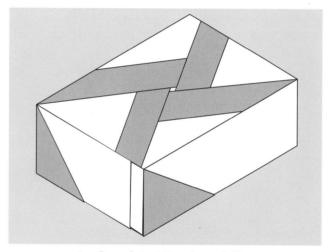

4. Completed Patchwork Box

Patchwork Effect: To create the two-tone effect shown in the illustration, use papers in two different colors and alternate them during the assembly.

GIFT BAG

Slipping a present into a pretty bag is quicker than wrapping it, and is especially convenient for odd shaped items. This bag is formed by folding gift wrap around a box or a few books in the way you would normally wrap a gift, but with one end left open. Use a good quality paper, or glue two thin sheets back to back.

You can be well prepared for the holiday season by making a few bags in different sizes ahead of time.

You need:

Gift wrap
1 yard (1 meter) cord or ribbon, Cereal or other box, Glue, Ruler, Pencil, Scissors, Paper Punch

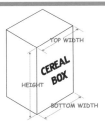

1. To find the correct height of the paper needed, measure the height of the box and add the widths across the top and bottom of the box.

2. To find the width of the paper needed, add together the widths of the front, back, and both sides of the box, plus 1" (3 cm) for an overlap. Cut the gift wrap to the appropriate size.

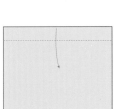

3. Fold down a long edge of the paper to an extent equal to the width of the top of the box.

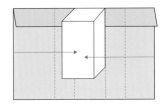

4a. Place the box on the wrong side of the paper, with the top of the box aligned with the folded edge.

4b. Wrap the paper around the box, letting it overlap in the middle. Make sharp creases over the box corners.

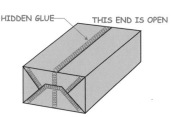

5a. Glue the overlapping edges together.

5b. Wrap the bottom of the box as you would normally wrap a gift box. Glue it closed.

5c. Remove the box.

6a. Punch holes 1" (2 cm) from the top edge of the bag, two holes on the front and two on the back, the same distance apart.

6b. Cut two pieces of cord each approximately 13" (35 cm) long.

6c. Guide the cords through the holes, making handles. Double-knot the four ends inside the bag.

6d. **Completed Gift Bag**

Decorations: If you make a bag from patterned gift wrap, you need only to tuck some colored tissue paper into the top of the bag. If you use plain paper, then there is no limit to the fun that you, your family, and friends can have decorating the bags with markers, confetti, or any odds and ends you have around.

STAND-UP FRAME

Here is another model designed by Laura Kruskal, who invented the Patchwork Box. The frame and stand are made from two separate pieces of paper.

You need:

Two pieces of paper, 8½" x 11" (or A4)

If paper is colored on only one side, begin with the white side facing up.

FOR THE FRAME

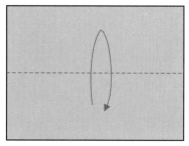

1a. Fold the paper in half the long way.
1b. Unfold the paper flat.

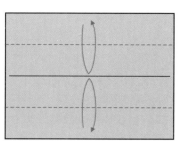

2a. Fold the long edges to the crease.
2b. Unfold the paper flat.

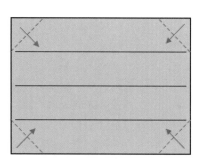

3. Fold the four corners to the nearest creases.

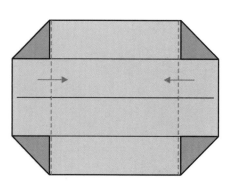

4. Valley fold on a line next to the corners as shown.

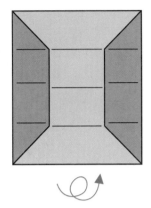

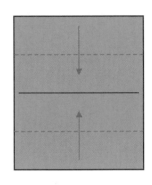

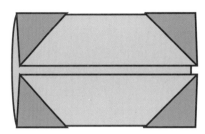

5. Turn the paper over.

6. Fold the top and bottom edges to the middle crease.

7. Completed Frame.

FOR THE STAND

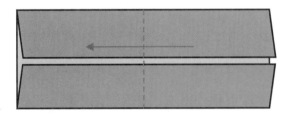

1. Using the second piece of paper, fold steps 1a, 1b, and 2a for the frame.
2. Fold the paper in half, the short way.

ASSEMBLY

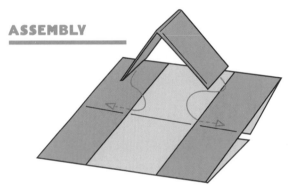

1. Place the frame with its back facing up. Slide the ends of the stand into the pockets of the frame.

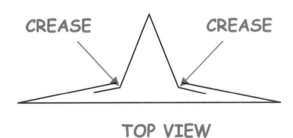

CREASE   CREASE

TOP VIEW

2. Top view of the assembled frame. Crease the stand where the ends will slide no further into the pockets. Insert a photo or postcard into the front of the frame, and stand it up.

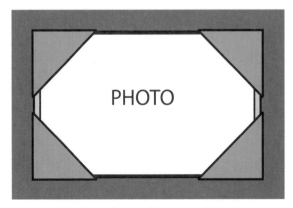

PHOTO

3. Completed Stand-up Frame
It can be set up horizontally or vertically. The stand can also be flattened for mailing.

TRIANGLE BOX

Triangle boxes can be filled with candies or nuts and set on a dinner table as favors, complementing the roundness of the plates. You may also find other occasions where they will work well.

The instructions will also work for making boxes from equilateral and other triangles.

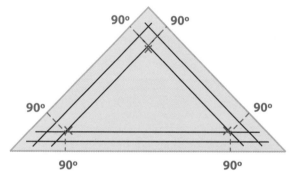

You need:

An 8" (20 cm) paper square cut from corner to corner into two triangles
Two paper clips
If the paper is colored on only one side, begin with the white side facing up.
For an open box, use only one triangle.

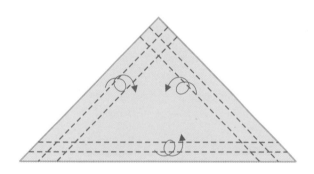

1. Fold each of the three edges ½" (1 cm) from the edge, then fold them over again. Unfold the paper flat.

2a. Form the upright corners of the box. The intersections of the creases are marked with Xs.

2b. From each X, make two creases at right angles to the outside edges. Unfold each time.

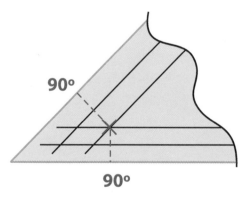

3. Enlarged view of step 2 in progress.

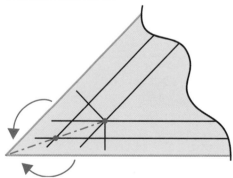

4a. Bisect each of the two acute corners of the triangle by pinching the edges together with a mountain fold, from the X to the corner.

4b. Unfold each time.

36

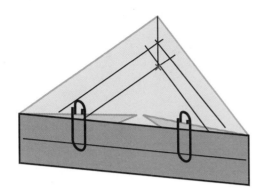

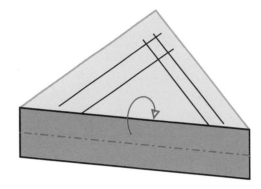

5a. Swing the two acute corners toward the middle of the long side, which will stand up.

5b. Hold them in place temporarily with paper clips.

6. Lock the long edge by doubling it over, and fasten it temporarily with the clips.

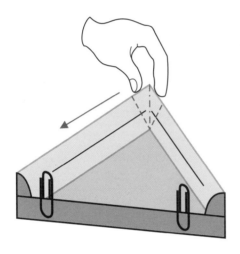

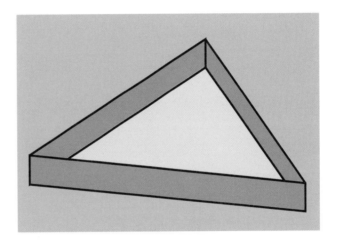

7a. Bisect the third, right-angle corner by pinching the edges together.

7b. Swing the corner over to one side.

7c. Lock the corner by folding over the two adjacent edges. You can now also lock the other two corners in neatly.

8. Completed Triangle Box

Covered Box: To prepare a covered box, use the other triangle piece and follow the same directions, but in step 1, fold the edges in slightly deeper. This will make it fit inside the first box, which will function as the lid.

MONEY BASKET

Turn a dollar bill into a basket for an unusual party favor. Although the fun is in converting real money, if it is not available, you may be able to find play money in toy and other stores. Or you can make the basket from a piece of letter paper cut in half the long way, or from larger rectangles.

You need:

A money bill

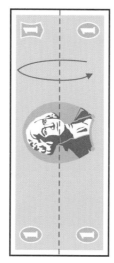

Ia. Fold the bill in half the long way.
Ib. Unfold the paper flat.

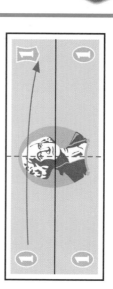

2. Fold the bill in half the short way.

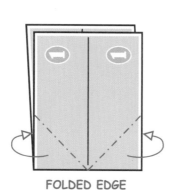

FOLDED EDGE

3a. Bring the corners from the folded edge to the middle crease.
3b. Unfold the corners and refold them, but this time in between the two main layers of paper. In origami language, this is called a reverse fold.

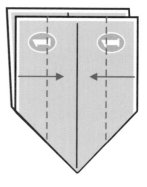

4a. On the front layer only, fold the outside edges to the middle crease.
4b. Turn the paper over and repeat on the back layer.

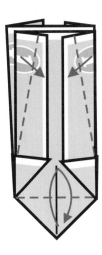

5a. Narrow the sides by folding them in at an angle, on the front and then on the back.

5b. Fold the bottom corner back and forth, to define the bottom of the basket, for later on.

6a. Open the basket by poking into the middle. Roll the handles over your finger (or a pen) to give them a slight curve.

6b. Insert the end of one handle into the end of the other handle.

6c. Sharpen the creases at the bottom of the basket.

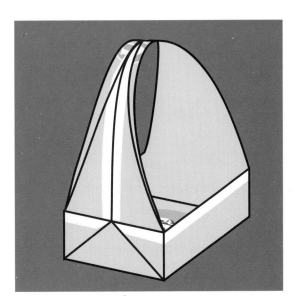

7. Completed Money Basket

COLOR CUBE

The Color Cube is an example of origami unit, or module, folding, in which several folded pieces are combined into one object. The unit was designed by the late Toshie Takahama of Japan. The Color Cube is used mostly as a fun decoration, although you can use it as a secret hiding place.

You need:

Six squares of paper: two red, two green, two yellow

If paper is colored on only one side, begin with the white side facing up. Fold all six squares in the same way.

FOLDING EACH UNIT

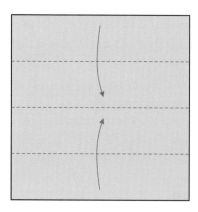

1a. Fold the square in half. Unfold.

1b. Fold the top and bottom edges to the middle crease.

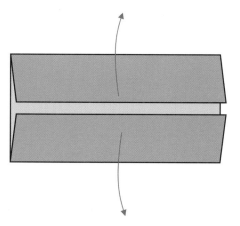

2. Unfold the paper flat.

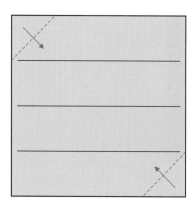

3. Fold the top left corner and the bottom right corner to the nearest crease.

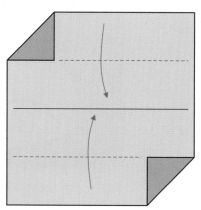

4. Refold on the creases made in step 1b.

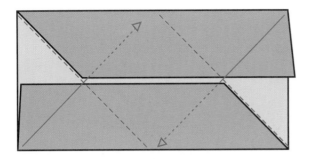

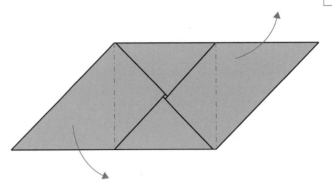

5a. Fold the left bottom corner under the top flap.

5b. Fold the top right corner under the bottom flap.

6. Mountain fold both ends, leaving a square in middle. Let the triangular ends hang loose.

ASSEMBLY

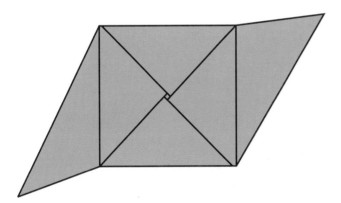

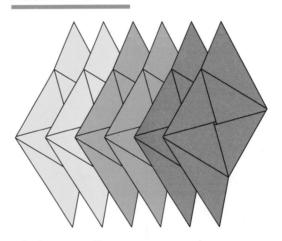

7. Completed unit

1. Line up all six units to make sure they are all folded alike.

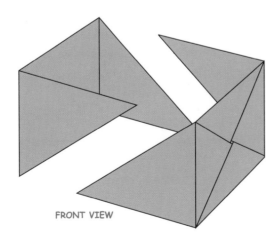

FRONT VIEW

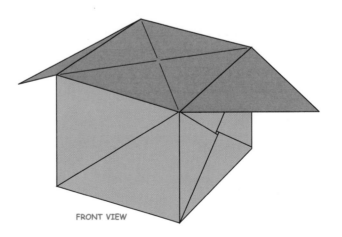

FRONT VIEW

2. Set up two green units facing each other, as shown.

3. Set a red unit on top, with the red triangles hanging over the square green sides.

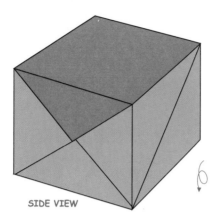

SIDE VIEW

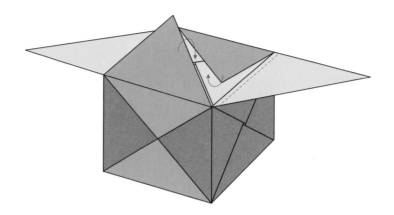

4a. Slide the red triangle into the green pocket.

4b. Repeat exactly on the opposite side.

4c. Turn the model upside down so that the red square is at the bottom.

4d. Repeat steps 3 through 4b.

5a. Slide the square side of a yellow unit under the two loose green triangles.

5b. Tuck the green triangles into the yellow pockets.

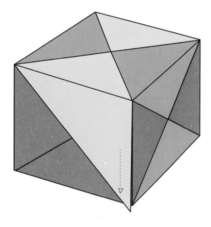

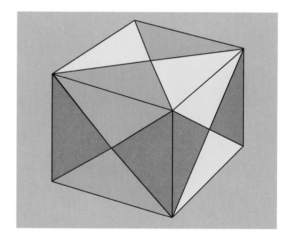

6a. Tuck the yellow triangles, which are hanging over the red squares, into the red pockets.

6b. Turn the cube upside down and repeat steps 5a through 6a on the opposite side.

7. Completed Color Cube
Note that each of the six sides is made up of four triangles in two different colors.

Color Choices: It is easier to use the suggested colors when you make your first Color Cube, but you can substitute your own color choices the next time.

Container: If you want to place something inside the cube, do so before completing step 6b.

Holiday Ornament: Fold the units from foil gift wrap and place a small bell inside.

Math Application: The Color Cube is a popular project in junior high and high school geometry classes. In greater numbers, the same units can be combined into much more complicated structures, presenting a challenge to ingenuity.

FLOWER GIFT WRAP

Nothing is simpler for wrapping cosmetic bottles, wine bottles, and other cylindrical containers, yet this method produces such a dramatic effect. It is accomplished with just two sheets of tissue paper of the same color or in two different, compatible colors.

You need:

Two sheets of tissue paper
Sticky tape, ribbon or raffia, scissors

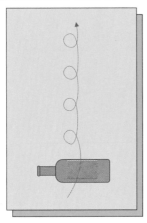

1a. Place the two sheets on top of each other, with the short edges 1" (2 cm) apart.

1b. Place the bottle near one of the shorter edges. Roll it up with the whole length of the paper.

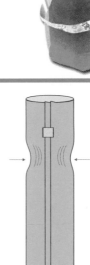

2a. Tape the ends together with sticky tape.

2b. Fold the end of the roll under the bottom of the bottle and tape it shut.

2c. Bunch the paper around the lowest part of the neck of the bottle and tie the ribbon or raffia tightly around it.

3a. Make two or three slits through all the layers of paper from the top down to the ribboned neck.

3b. Beginning with the outer layer, pull the paper down, twisting the first layer to one side and the next layer to the other side, forming a flower.

4. Completed Flower Gift Wrap

Other Containers: For wrapping jam jars and other round containers, use paper about 5" (12 cm) wider than the height of the jar.

Cuff: For an extra touch, wrap the bottom of the cylinder with colored corrugated paper.

STAR BASKET

Teachers of origami favor this traditional Japanese basket, as it is easy to teach and students enjoy the results.

You need:

A *paper square*

If paper is colored on only one side, begin with the white side facing up.

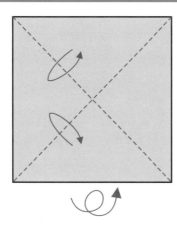

1a. Fold the square from corner to corner in both directions. Unfold each time.

1b. Turn the paper over.

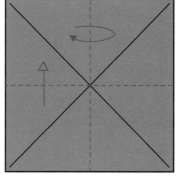

2a. Fold the paper in half and unfold.

2b. Fold the paper in half the other way and leave it folded.

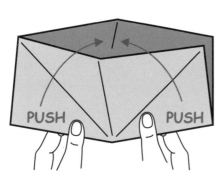

3. Grasp the paper with both hands at the folded edge in the exact positions shown in the diagram. Move your hands up and toward each other in the direction of the arrows until the paper is formed into a square. Place it flat on the table.

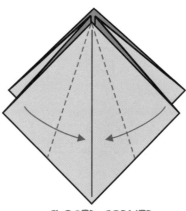

OPEN CORNER

CLOSED CORNER

4a. Make sure the square has two flaps on each side. If you have only one flap on one side and three flaps on the other, flip one flap over. In origami language, this is called a square or preliminary base.

4b. Place the square with the open corner away from you. Fold the outer edges of the front flaps to the middle crease.

4c. Turn the paper over and repeat with the two flaps on the back.

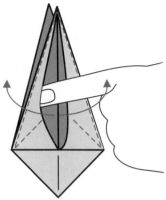

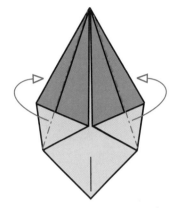

5a. Poke your finger into the pocket on the left, spread the two layers apart and squash flat. See the next diagram. Repeat with the right pocket.

5b. Turn the paper over and repeat on the back.

6a. Mountain fold the top layer on both sides.
6b. Repeat on the back.

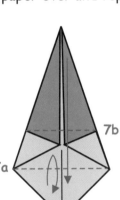

7a. Fold the bottom corner up, first to the front and then to the back, making a sharp crease. Unfold into the previous position.
7b. Fold the top corner down on the front and repeat on the back.

8a. Fold the right flap over to the left, like turning the page of a book. In origami language, this is called a book fold.
8b. Repeat on the back, again folding from right to left.

POKE IN HERE

9. Poke your finger into the top and spread the bottom apart.

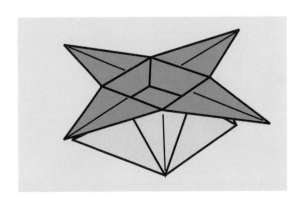

10. **Completed Star Basket**

TRIANGLE GIFT BOX

I was inspired to create this box after seeing a shopping bag in this shape. Of course it was pieced and glued, but I thought I could design a similar shape within the confines of origami. The pattern begins with pre-folding a grid, which provides all the necessary creases to form the box. The box can be kept closed by cutting a slit or attaching Velcro patches.

You need:

A piece of paper, 9" x 12"
Ruler, Pencil, Craft Knife
If paper is colored on only one side, begin with the white side facing up.

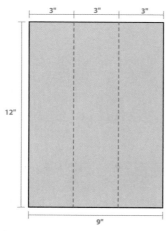

1. Make two vertical valley folds 3" apart. Unfold the paper flat.

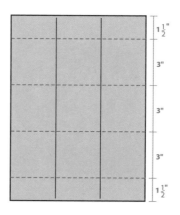

2. Make four horizontal valley folds, as shown, beginning 1½" from the short edges and at 3" intervals in between.

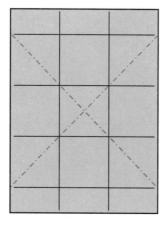

3. Make two diagonal mountain folds across the nine squares. Unfold after each crease.

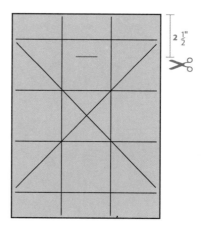

4. Completed grid. Cut a 1½" wide slit with the craft knife, 2¼" down from the top edge and across the middle of the paper.
Caution: Children need adult help.

TRIANGLE GIFT BOX

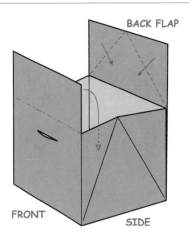

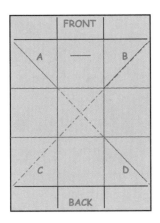

5a. Make valley and mountain folds as shown. The central square becomes the bottom of the box.

5b. Overlap the diagonal mountain folds A and B across the middle square.

5c. Overlap the diagonal mountain folds C and D. You will have a box.

6a. Fold the front flap to the inside.

6b. Fold the corners of the back flap toward the inside of the box.

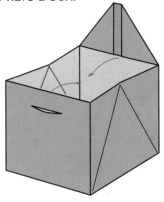

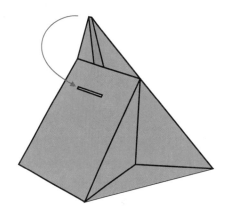

7. At the top bring the back and front of the box together. Push in both sides so they cave in.

8. Side view. Lock the box by tucking the back flap into the slit on the front.

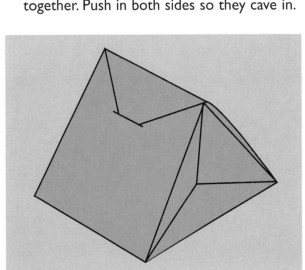

9. Completed Triangle Gift Box

Sizes: For this box, construction paper is suitable and comes in the right size. The suggested size of paper results in a 3" box. You can make other sizes from papers in the proportion of 3 x 4.

Pocket book: The pocket book in the photo is made from a piece of gift wrap 21" x 28" (51 cm x 68 cm). The front flap is folded into the fancy shape with a diagonal mountain fold, followed by a valley fold, and then secured with Velcro patches. The strap can be attached to the sides of the box with staples, glue, or tape.

FIVE HAPPINESS BOWL

This traditional bowl has a symbolic meaning in Asian culture, in which numbers play an important role. Its five compartments represent the five elements of wood, fire, earth, metal, and water. Serving almonds, other nuts, or candy on special occasions in Five Happiness Bowls has added significance.

You need:

A paper square (paper colored on both sides is best)

If paper is colored on only one side, begin with the colored side facing up.

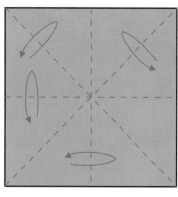

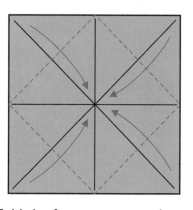

1a. Fold the square in half in both directions. Unfold both times.

1b. Fold from corner to corner, in both directions. Unfold both times.

2. Fold the four corners to the center.

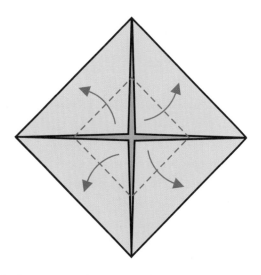

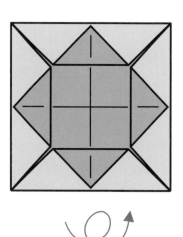

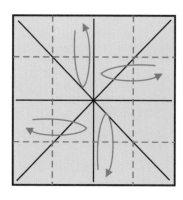

3. In origami language, this shape is called a blintz base. Fold the four corners out to the edges.

4. Turn the paper over.

5. Valley fold the four edges to the center, unfolding the paper after each fold.

Step 6 in progress

6a. Sharply crease the middle square, created by the valley folds, to define the bottom of the bowl.

6b. Pinch each of the four corners between your thumb and forefinger, making valley folds.

6c. Push the four corners to the outside and flatten them. See diagram.

7a. Fold the four outside corners to the middle. Unfold each time.

7b. On the same creases, fold the four corners to the middle again, but this time between the two layers of paper. In origami language, this is called a reverse fold.

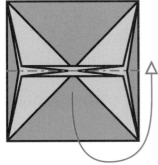

8. Mountain fold the paper in half, to the back.

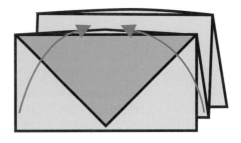

9. Place the paper exactly as shown. Push the hidden side edges to the middle, making reverse folds.

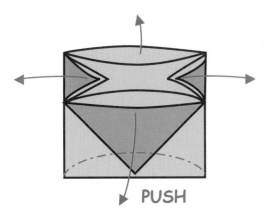

PUSH

10a. Open each of the four pockets by pulling the outside layer away; at the same time push on the bottom of the pocket to curve it.

10b. Shape the top and bottom of the bowl. It helps to poke a toothpick into both corners of each pocket.

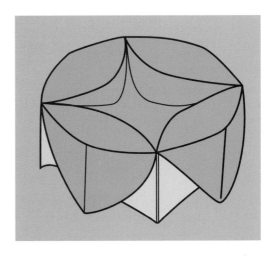

11. Completed Five Happiness Bowl

MYSTERY BOX

Everyone eyes this box with a puzzled look, as it is very intriguing. For your first try, I recommend a square cut from an 8½" x 11" (A4) piece of printing or bond paper, which will produce a box approximately 2", or 5 cm across.

You need:

A paper square

If paper is colored on only one side, begin with the white side facing up.
With this box, it is very important to make very sharp creases with each fold.

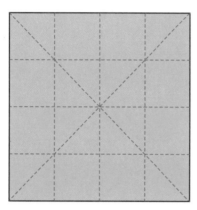

1a. Fold the square in half both ways. Unfold the paper both times.

1b. Fold on both diagonals. Unfold both times.

1c. Fold all four edges to the middle creases; unfold the paper both times.

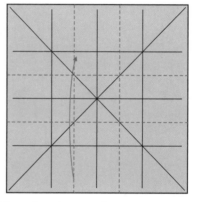

2. Fold each edge to the third crease away from it. Unfold each time.

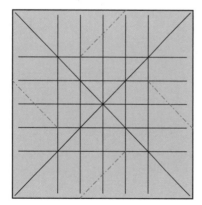

3. Make four mountain folds, as shown. Unfold each time.

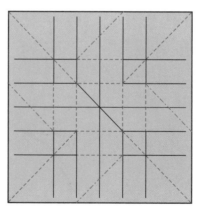

4. On the existing creases, make extra sharp mountain and valley folds only on the sections shown.

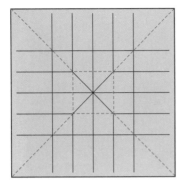

5. Shape the bottom of the box with four valley folds around the four central squares. At the same time, pinch the corners to the outside on the existing diagonal creases.

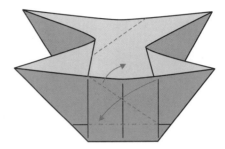

6. Push the creases made in step 3 toward the middle of the box, at the same time forming the upright sides of the box. Four triangles will form in the middle. Arrange them so that the left side of one is on top of the right side of the adjacent one. See the next diagram.

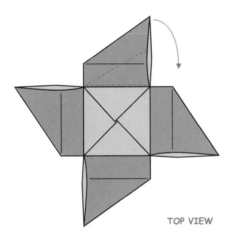

TOP VIEW

7a. Twist one of the wings with a slanted mountain fold to the right.

7b. Then make a valley fold to make the wing stand upright.

7c. Repeat steps 7a and 7b with the other three wings.

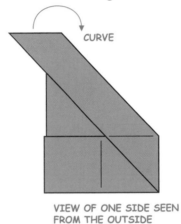

CURVE

VIEW OF ONE SIDE SEEN
FROM THE OUTSIDE

8. Interweave all four top corners of the wings by pushing them toward the middle. Each angled corner fits under the next wing, leaving a hole in the middle.

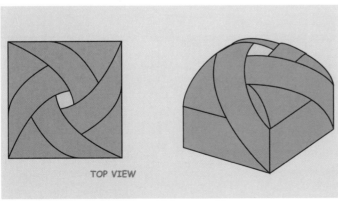

TOP VIEW

9. Completed Mystery Box

Tip: After you have opened and closed the box two or three times, the creases will settle in and the box will reform easily.

HEXAGON BOX

Here is another example of unit folding, this time for making a hexagonal 5½" (13 cm) box using two rectangular pieces of paper each for the bottom and lid of the box. It is a variation created by Thoki Yenn of Denmark of an original design by Shuzo Fujimoto of Japan.

You need:

Four pieces of paper, 8½" x 11" (or A4)

If paper is colored on only one side, begin with the colored side facing up. Fold all four pieces the same way.

FOLDING EACH UNIT

1a. Valley fold the paper into quarters, the short way.
1b. Unfold the paper flat.
1c. Turn the paper over.

2. Fold the bottom right corner to the first crease, beginning the fold at the bottom edge of the second crease.

3. Fold the top edge to this corner of the paper, leaving a tiny gap (about ⅛") between them.

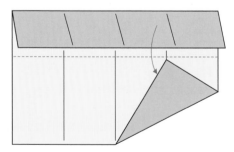

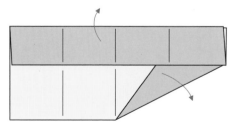

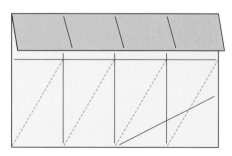

4. Fold the edge over again. This will form the sides of the box.

5. Unfold the last crease and unfold the angled crease made in step 2.

6. Valley fold and unfold all four rectangles diagonally, from the lower left corner to the upper right corner.

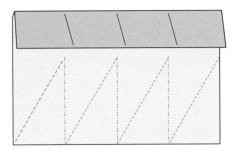

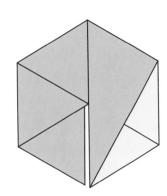

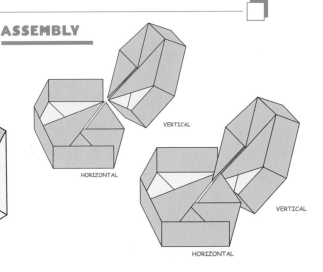

VERTICAL

HORIZONTAL

VERTICAL

HORIZONTAL

7a. Grasp the paper on the slanted valley fold on the extreme right and push it to the left along the adjacent mountain fold.

7b. Repeat step 7a with the other three valley folds.

7c. Crease the upright corners on the sides of the box sharply.

8. Completed unit, looking down at the pattern inside the box.

1. You need two units for the bottom of the box and two units for the lid. Hold one unit horizontally with your left hand and the other unit vertically with your right hand. The vertical unit must have three equilateral triangles at the top. Slide the openings of two units into each other along the slits in the bottom. Then twist the combined units into a box shape. You should have six equilateral triangles on the inside of the box.

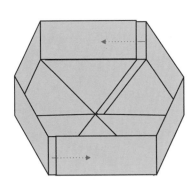

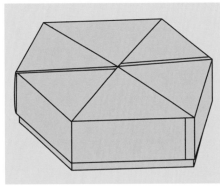

3. Completed Hexagon Box

2a. The sides at both ends have two layers. Loosen the corner of the outside end and fold it over the one on the inside. You have to slide both units a little apart temporarily. Repeat with the opposite ends.

2b. Place the lid on top of the bottom of the box.

Shorter Lid: For a shorter edge around the lid, cut off 1½" (5 cm) from one of the long edges of the two pieces of paper before you begin. Now it is 7" x 11". Then follow the instructions for folding the box.

Other Sizes: Almost any size rectangles can be used to fold Hexagon Boxes. Experiment with different sizes to achieve different diameters and heights.

FOUR THIRSTY BIRDS

Four birds will admire whatever you decide to put in this amusing box designed by David Lister, former president of the British Origami Society. It is best to attempt Four Thirsty Birds after you have folded some of the previous models in the book.

You need:

A paper square 8" (20 cm) or larger

If paper is colored on only one side, begin with the white side facing up.

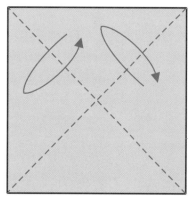

1a. Fold a square from corner to corner, in both directions.

1b. Unfold the paper both times.

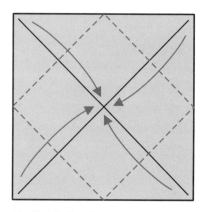

2. Fold the four corners to the center.

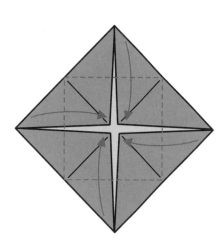

3. In origami language, this is called a blintz base. Fold the four corners to the center again.

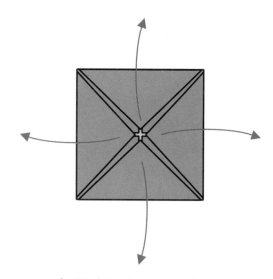

4. Unfold the paper flat.

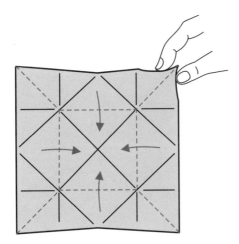

5a. Place the paper with the white side up. Crease the valley folds forming the middle square sharply to define the bottom of the box.

5b. Pinch each of the four corners between your thumb and forefinger.

5c. Press the four edges to meet in the middle; the four corners will rise up.

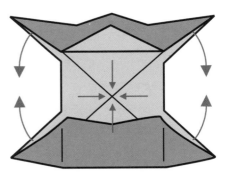

6. Guide the four corners to the outside to lie flat.

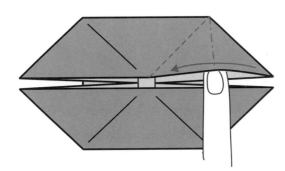

7a. Poke your finger between the two layers and spread it apart. Push the corner of the paper down to the center to form a small square, and press it flat. In origami language this is called a squash fold.

7b. Repeat with the other three corners.

8. On each of the four squares, fold the cut edges to the diagonal crease.

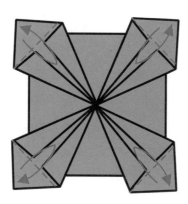

9. Fold the four outside corners over the triangles you just folded. Unfold them.

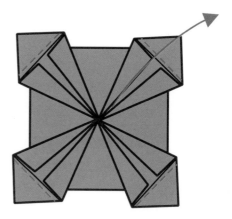

10a. In the center of the paper find a corner of the original paper square. Lift it up to the outside, on the crease made in step 9. The sides open up and then move together to form a diamond. In origami language, this is called a petal fold.

10b. Repeat with the other three corners.

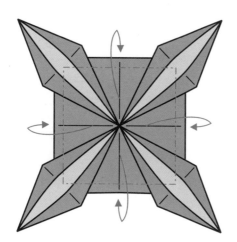

11. Mountain fold and unfold creases between the centers of the diamonds.

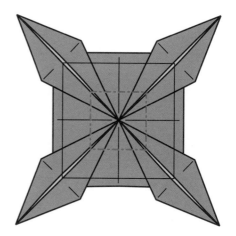

12. Valley fold and unfold, halfway between the new mountain folds and the center of the paper. This defines the bottom of the box.

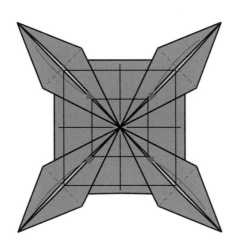

13. Fold the four corners in. They will become the birds.

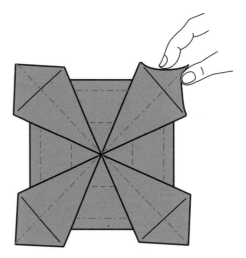

14. Pinch each of the four corners between your thumb and forefinger; at the same time reshape the mountain and valley folds made in steps 11 and 12. See the next diagram for the result.

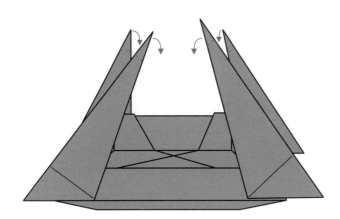

15. Fold the four bird beaks by pulling each corner forward and then pinching the back of the head to make it stay in position. (This will make reverse folds.)

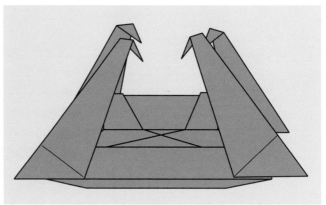

16. Completed Four Thirsty Birds

The Birds Can Drink: **When you press on the back of a bird, it seems to be taking a drink.**

ROUND BOWL

Not many origami models are truly round, which makes this bowl unusual. When you accomplish folding it, after following its many steps, you can consider yourself a capable paper-folder. The model incorporates several forms that recur frequently in traditional paperfolding and are described with technical terms such as triangle or waterbomb base, petal fold, and frog base. As you proceed you will be following a mini-course in origami.

You need:

A paper square between 8" and 10" (20 cm–25 cm)

If paper is colored on only one side, begin with the colored side facing up.

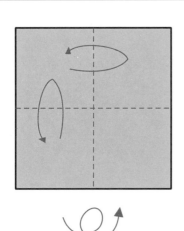

1a. Fold the square in half, both ways. Unfold the paper flat each time.

1b. Turn the paper over.

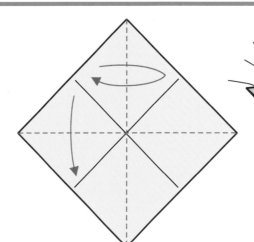

2a. Fold the paper from corner to corner and unfold.

2b. Fold corner to corner in the other direction and leave folded. You will have a triangle.

3. Grasp the paper with both hands at the folded edge in the exact positions shown in the diagram. Move your hands toward each other until the paper forms into a smaller triangle. Place it flat on the table.

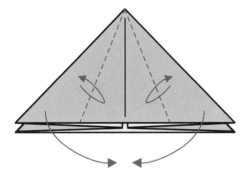

4a. Make sure the triangle has two flaps on each side. If you have only one flap one one side and three flaps on the other, flip one flap over. In origami language, this is called a triangle or waterbomb base.

4b. Fold the outside edges of the front flaps to the middle. Unfold them.

4c. Fold again on the same creases but this time bring the paper in between the two layers of paper. In origami language, this is called a reverse fold.

4d. Turn the model over and repeat steps 4b through 4d on the back.

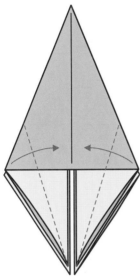

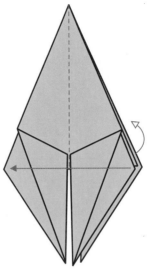

5a. Fold the short outer edges of the front flaps to the middle.

5b. Turn the model over and repeat on the back.

6a. Fold the right outer corner over to the left, like turning the page of a book. In origami language, this is called a book fold.

6b. Repeat on the back, again folding the outer corner from right to left.

6c. Repeat steps 5a and 5b on the front and the back.

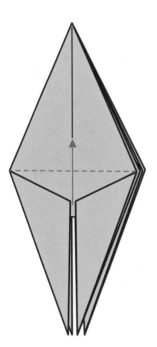

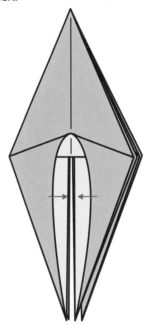

7a. Lift the edge hidden between the two flaps up in the direction of the arrow and make a valley fold, as shown.

7b. The sides open up as you do this and then meet in the middle. In origami language, this is called a petal fold.

8a. This shows step 7 in progress.

8b. Turn the model over and repeat steps 7a and 7b on the back.

8c. Make two book folds and make two more petal folds.

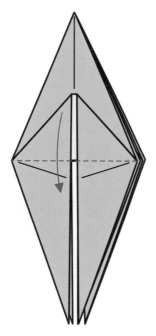

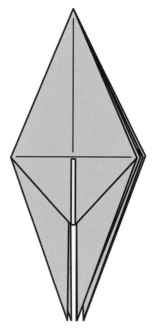

9. In origami language, this is called a frog base. Fold the corners of the petal folds down on all four sides.

10. Unfold the paper completely.

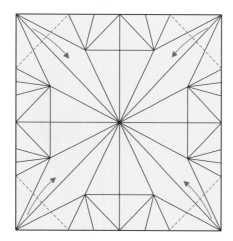

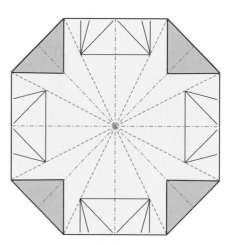

11. Valley fold all four corners toward the center, as shown. Note where the creases begin along the edges.

12. Reform the paper into the frog base on the existing creases. *Hint*: Begin by folding alternating mountain and valley folds, as shown.

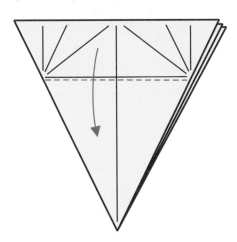

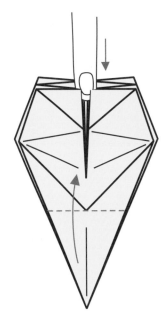

13. Step 12 in progress. Pull the middle point on each of the top edges down to re-form the base.

14a. Arrange the paper so that there are four flaps on each side.

14b. Fold the bottom corner up, first to the front, then to the back. Unfold.

14c. Poke your finger into the top of the bowl to open it up.

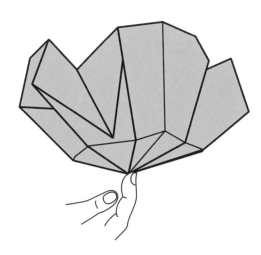

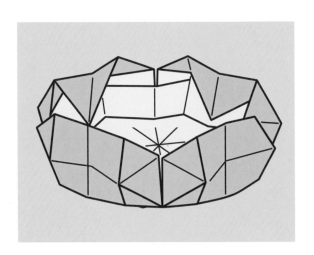

15. The crease made in step 14b will define the bottom of the bowl when you press on the center of the paper.

16. **Completed Round Bowl**

ONE-PIECE BOX

This hinged box, made from a single sheet of stiff paper, collapses magically into place after some preliminary creasing. It was designed by V'Ann Cornelius, vice-president of OrigamiUSA.

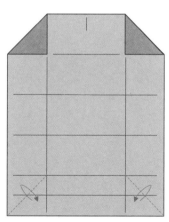

You need:

A piece of paper 8" x 10" (20 cm x 25 cm)

If paper is colored on only one side, begin with the white side facing up.

1a. Pinch a small crease at the halfway point of the short top edge.

1b. Fold the two long edges to meet at the halfway mark.

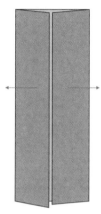

2. Unfold the paper flat. In origami language this is called a book fold.

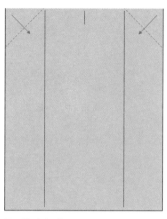

3. Fold the two top corners to the creases.

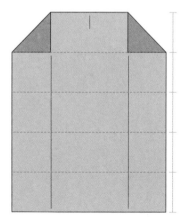

4. Valley fold the paper into five equal parts, using the folded corners as the measurement, unfolding each time.

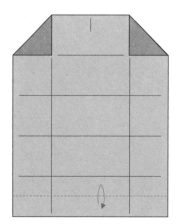

5a. Valley fold the bottom edge up to the nearest crease.

5b. Unfold.

6. Make valley folds on both bottom corners, as shown, unfolding them both times.

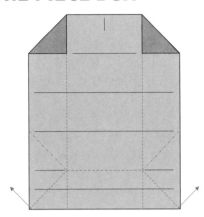

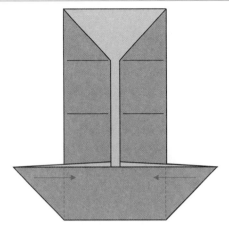

7. Fold the long edges to the middle, on the existing creases, but bring the bottom corners up and to the outside, on the creases made in step 6. See the next diagram.

8. Fold both outside corners to the middle.

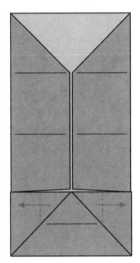

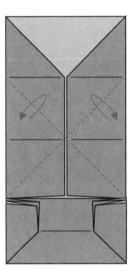

9a. Make two valley folds, as shown.
9b. Unfold these two creases and refold them in between the two layers of paper. In origami language, this is called a reverse fold.

10. Make two valley folds, as shown, unfolding them both times.

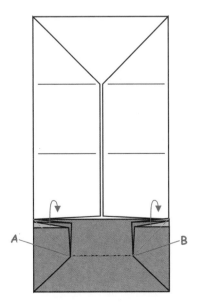

11. Lock the bottom of the box by grasping the long layer and the next two layers at each corner and pushing them inside. The corners will automatically form on the existing creases. Pay special attention to the mountain folds marked A and B.
The sides of the box rise as you perform step 11.

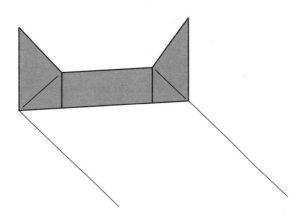

12. Inside view of the bottom of the box.

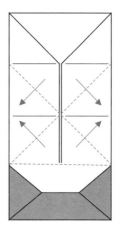

13a. Outside view.

13b. Bend up the back of the box along the horizontal crease closest to the bottom.

13c. Reinforce the creases made on the inside layers in step 10.

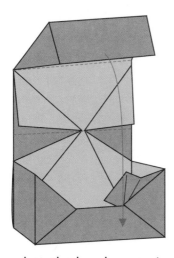

14. Complete the box by creasing the two upper horizontal folds sharply. The top goes over the front.

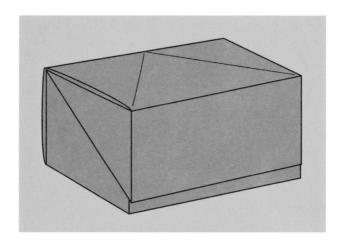

15. **Completed One-Piece Box**
Keep it closed with a ribbon.

The box can be made from any size rectangle in the ratio of 4 x 5.